POLAND'S NOBLE SON

Poland's Noble Son

Life of St. Stanislaus Kostka

Written by
the Daughters of St. Paul
and
Maxine Mayer

Illustrated by
Maxine Mayer

St. Paul Books & Media

Library of Congress Cataloging in Publication Data

Main Entry under title:
Poland's noble son.

Summary: A biography of a patron saint of Poland, whose childhood
desire for holiness led him to have visions of angels and the Virgin Mary
before he met his early death.
   1. Kostka, Stanislaus, Saint, 1550-1568—Juvenile literature. 2. Christian saints—Poland—Biography—Juvenile literature. [1. Kostka, Stanislaus,
Saint, 1550-1568. 2. Saints]
I. Mayer, Maxine, ill. II. Daughters of St. Paul.
BX4700.S7P64   1984   282'.092'4   [B]   [92]   83-18887

ISBN 0-8198-5814-5 cloth
      0-8198-5815-3 paper

Printed in the U.S.A., by the Daughters of St. Paul
50 St. Paul's Ave., Boston, MA 02130

The Daughters of St. Paul are an international congregation of women
religious serving the Church with the communications media.

CONTENTS

CHAPTER 1

A NOBLE'S SON

Lord John Kostka paced the hall of the large, drafty castle. Maids rushed here and there, back and forth, in and out of his wife's room.

"Will they never stop and tell me how Lady Margaret is?" he asked himself impatiently.

Finally he stepped squarely in front of a young maid rushing out of the door.

"How is Lady Margaret?" he demanded.

Startled, she looked up into the worried face of Lord John.

"Don't worry," she answered kindly, "I think very soon you will have a new Kostka in the family. And Lady Margaret is doing fine!" she added as she hurried on down the hall.

Just when he thought he could stand the suspense no longer, he heard the welcome cry of a baby. Tensely, he waited for them to call him to his wife's bedside.

"Lord John," one of the maids finally called from the door, "come see your new son! Mother and child are both doing fine!"

Greatly relieved, he went straight to his wife. There, snuggled in her arms was a tiny, newborn baby son. Lady Margaret looked into her proud husband's eyes. He was a big, gruff man with a heart as soft as cotton. She smiled when she realized how worried he had been. Big Lord John, who was afraid of neither man nor beast, stood like a gentle lamb before the miracle of life.

"Isn't he beautiful, John?"

"He's going to be a handsome man, Margaret. He's a Kostka, with noble blood and a strong heart."

"Would you like to hold him?" Margaret offered. She knew that her husband wanted very much to hold him, but he was always fearful of his own strength. He felt so insecure and clumsy with something so small and precious.

One of the maids took the baby and placed him in his father's arms. His big hands engulfed his small son and the maid shifted the infant and rearranged John's hand in the proper position.

"There, Lord John, you have to hold his head up like this."

In these matters, certainly the women knew best. He looked at the child in his arms.

"Why Margaret, he looks just like me!"

Margaret nodded and smiled broadly, humoring his imagined likeness to the wrinkled, red newborn baby.

"Will you begin preparations for his baptism, John? This little one is waiting for the grace of God."

"I'll start right away," he assured her as he handed the precious bundle to one of the maids. "He is the son of a noble and he will soon be a child of God as well. We'll call him 'Stanislaus,' after the great bishop and martyr. You rest now, Margaret, and don't worry about a thing."

He squeezed her hand for a moment more, then turned quickly and left the room. It wouldn't do to have the maids see the great Lord John with a tear in his eye.

October of 1550 was special in the Kostka castle. The very day after Stanislaus was born, messengers on horseback rode throughout Poland announcing the coming baptism. Everyone was invited by Lord John to rejoice with the family.

Soon a procession of nobles in feather plumes and furs began to converge on the castle. Great ladies in rich horse-drawn carriages arrived with their maids and servants. Every guest room in the castle was filled and a neighboring castle had offered to keep some of the guests as well.

There were games and parties and hunts to occupy the guests for a few days to give everyone a chance to arrive. Lady Margaret, with little Stanislaus in her arms, had a steady stream of visitors. Each brought a gift to the child and laid it on a table especially prepared for that purpose.

"Lady Margaret," one guest said, "my gift must remain outside."

"Outside! But why? I can have the servants bring it in if that will help," Lady Margaret replied.

"Oh no! I'm sure you would prefer me to leave it outside," answered the smiling guest with a twinkle in his eye. "It's an Arabian pony! It wouldn't look at all good on that table!"

Everyone joined in the laughter. Little Stanislaus slept and cried and ate through it all, never realizing all this celebrating was for his benefit.

After all the guests had arrived, a procession was formed to go to the little village church of St. Adalbert. As they made their way to the church they sang hymns to the Blessed Mother. Stanislaus was carried in a little cradle, well packed amid soft blankets.

At the church, the ceremonies of baptism were performed by Father John, the parish priest. After the waters of baptism had made Stanislaus a child of God, his godfather, Andrew, took him and laid him at the foot of the altar as a sign of consecration to God.

The procession back to the castle was a joyous celebration. That night there was a big banquet in the largest room of the castle. Everyone was happy. Dish after dish of delicious food was placed before the guests. At the front gate of the castle, food was given out to the peasants and the poor people. No one was supposed to be hungry on that night. Even the servants had a banquet of their own after all the guests and the poor had been taken care of.

The Kostkas were devout Catholic Christians. They wanted their children to have a strong faith. From their earliest years the children were taught to pray, to be devout at Mass, and to try to correct bad habits.

"The flowers show us how beautiful God must be."

CHAPTER 2

BEES AND BEARS

"Mother, how beautiful are all these flowers, the trees, and the sky."

"Yes, Stanislaus, and they show us how beautiful God must be, because He made them."

"I love God very much, Mother, and I want to do something special for Him in my life."

"Well, Stanislaus, you pray hard and try to be good always, and God is very pleased. He will show you what to do."

Mrs. Kostka herself prayed very much for her son, who would not have to wait too long for God's answer.

Stanislaus had a very sensitive nature which he had received from his mother, who was very devout and gentle. She understood Stanislaus more than anyone else in the family did. How many times Stanislaus and his mother walked through the fields and among the hills of Rostkow.

Poland is a tiny country—thirty times smaller than the United States. It is full of beautiful scenery—mountains and hills, lakes and rivers, vast

17

fields—the kind of nature that reminds people about God and makes them happy to be alive.

The people of Poland adopted Christianity in the year 966 A.D., and have remained loyal to the Faith through all their struggles ever since. Even in Stanislaus' time, there had been a great many holy people from this small country. In fact, its great King Casimir had been canonized just thirty years before Stanislaus Kostka was born in the castle of Rostkow.

It was a common practice to consecrate babies to the Blessed Mother, usually at the time they were baptized. We are quite sure this was done for Stanislaus. Its effects showed in his life from a very early age.

One day, there was a certain guest at the castle. Little Stanislaus was sitting off to the side, looking at some books, while the gentleman talked to his father. All of a sudden the guest exclaimed, "Is Stanislaus all right?" as the little boy collapsed into a heap on the floor.

"Oh, yes, he'll be all right," his father replied, picking the boy up. "I'm sorry. We usually warn our guests, but I forgot to tell you that Stanislaus faints when someone uses bad language."

Stanislaus and his older brother, Paul, were always together. They were less than two years apart and were forever getting into mischief. All the servants felt just as responsible for them as their parents did. Everyone was free to correct

"I forgot to tell you thaf Stanislaus faints
when someone uses bad language."

them at any time. Sometimes they would try to slip away unnoticed, but there were so many servants that it was nearly impossible.

If the boys failed to study their lessons, or got their good clothes muddy, or showed up late for lunch, the whole castle was likely to know about it by evening. But everything was done in love. The servants were very fond of the Kostka children and they knew it.

The servants were the boys' first teachers. On snowy winter nights the boys sat with them around the fireplace and heard tales of adventure and bravery. There were stories of knights in shining armor rescuing lovely ladies from impossible towers. Rabbits, wolves and foxes could suddenly talk, and Paul and Stanislaus would be immersed in the world of make-believe.

They often went with Lord John to oversee the farming. They would mount their ponies and follow their father's spirited horse through the fields.

Everyone seemed to like Lord John. The peasants would look up from their work and wave. A farmer's wife would step out of her tiny cottage and meet them in the road. In each hand she would have a little cake for Lord John's two sons. He would make Paul and Stanislaus get off their ponies to receive the cakes and thank the good woman. The farmers would ask Lord John's advice and they would discuss crops, the harvest and market prices.

Sometimes the boys would grow tired on these trips, but they had been taught that a Kostka does his duty no matter what the cost. Never did a sign of tiredness or rudeness escape their father. They were reminded more than once that they should be grateful to God, for all they had was given by God.

The children learned ancient common sense from the peasants and servants. "A guest in the home means God in the home," they were told whenever someone came to visit. Visitors were to be treated with the greatest politeness and kindness, just as one would treat Jesus if He came.

Even a poor beggar at the kitchen door was treated with politeness and generosity. "Christ is hidden under the cloak of a poor man. Whatever you do for the poor," they were taught, "Christ considers done for Him."

"Paul, Stanislaus!" their father called one day. They came running to see what new adventure lay ahead. Studies were over for the day and they were ready for anything.

"I thought you boys might like to go with the 'honey man.' He said he would be happy to take you along. Try to be back by dark and see that you obey and behave as Kostkas."

The "honey man" was very important. Honey was the only thing they had to sweeten food with, since there was no sugar in Poland at that time. The "honey man" kept the castle and the village supplied with honey he would collect in the forests.

The "honey man" smiled as the boys ran to get their ponies. In a short time they were back, almost as excited over a trip to the woods as their ponies seemed to be.

"How do you know where to find the honey?" Paul wanted to know.

"Well," answered their guide while they rode along a forest path, "you know that bears love honey. First I find where the bears are, then I trail them to the honey. They do all the searching for me."

"Aren't bears dangerous?" Stanislaus asked, remembering all the stories he had heard around the fireplace.

"Very dangerous if you are alone, unarmed and walking. But I usually have my faithful horse, a good sword, and a reasonable amount of caution. I've already scouted this area and I think we will find honey in that clump of trees ahead."

Their eyes were just getting accustomed to the dim light of the forest. The trail became narrower and narrower. Soon they had to ride single file. Suddenly the "honey man's" horse reared up in fright. While he was trying to get control of his horse, Stanislaus' pony shied to the left so quickly that he nearly lost his balance. There, right in front of them on the path was a bear! For an eternal moment everyone froze, even the horses. At first the bear looked angry and ready to attack. But then, as everyone remained still and he realized that these new creatures in his forest did not seem to be much of a threat, he calmly ambled off into the woods.

Everyone breathed a sigh of relief. The boys were a bit shaken, but they were anxious to get the honey and go home to tell about their adventure.

"I have to compliment you, boys," their leader began, trying to put them at ease. "You handled your ponies like professional hunters. And neither of you acted afraid. You stood your ground as true Kostkas. That bear didn't dare attack such brave foes! Your father will be proud of you both."

The boys felt much better after all the praise and they were ready to follow their leader's directions. They split up and each took a small area. They examined each tree carefully, looking for a honeycomb. Bees buzzed around as a sign that they were close.

"Here it is!" shouted Stanislaus. He could hardly believe he had been the one to spot it. High up between two branches was a very large honeycomb teeming with bees.

"Won't we get stung if we try to take it down?" questioned Paul.

"We certainly could! But there's a little trick we can use. Help me gather some green branches and pile them around the tree."

The boys jumped off their ponies and began gathering and piling branches. When they had a good amount, the "honey man" set fire to the branches. Because they were green, the branches refused to blaze up and just sent up billows of smoke. The boys watched amazed as the bees came buzzing out of the comb and flew away as fast as they could.

"They don't like the smoke," explained the "honey man." When the smoke died down, he climbed up to the comb and cut it off the branch. The tree was unharmed.

"When the bees come back," he chuckled, "they will have to build a new house. But that doesn't seem to bother them. They are perfect little builders and their know-how comes straight from God."

On the way home, the "honey man" explained the fascinating story of bees and gave them more information on the habits of bears. The boys didn't realize it, but that day they had had a real lesson about the secrets of nature. From then on they had a much greater appreciation for honey and for bees.

As time went on, Paul and Stanislaus showed themselves to be very different from each other. Paul became very wild and willing to do anything for fun and excitement. Stanislaus also enjoyed fun and games, but he was more serious about his studies and about keeping God's law. Many times Paul thought Stanislaus was being good just to show him up. He would often run past his younger brother, bumping him just hard enough to make him fall down, but not so hard as to hurt him badly

Many times Paul played too rough with Stanislaus.

and get himself punished. Stanislaus always laughed shakily, got up and brushed himself off. He silently forgave Paul and prayed for the strength to be a good sport and to be able to keep up with the other boys.

CHAPTER 3

WHAT'S IN A NAME?

Stanislaus had never given much thought to his name. He had always been called Stanislaus and had never wondered about the reason why. One day he and Paul started talking about names. They had a new hunting hound and were trying to agree on what to call it. Somehow they began discussing their own names. Soon an argument developed, as each insisted his own name was the best.

"My name is best because it is in the Bible," boasted Paul, whose patron saint was the great Apostle Paul who wrote some of the New Testament. "I never saw the name Stanislaus in the Bible."

Stanislaus was silent, trying to think of a good answer. It was true. Paul's name was in the Bible and his wasn't! But not wanting to let Paul win the argument, he insisted that his name was still the best and he was going to find out why from their mother. They both marched off to find Lady Margaret.

Lady Margaret was sewing in the blue room, so-called because of blue draperies on the windows. When she saw the grim faces on her two boys as they walked in, she knew they had been arguing. They heatedly explained their discussion.

"Aren't you two ashamed?" Lady Margaret asked as the boys began to look at the floor. "Imagine, arguing over such a silly thing! As if God had not given each of you the best name he could have!"

It hadn't seemed so silly a few minutes ago, but now it did look pretty foolish as Lady Margaret continued.

"Now, both of you say you're sorry and shake hands. If one of you were a little humble, he would have given in. But since you are both proud, you argue."

By now the boys were thoroughly ashamed, and they shook hands. Stanislaus decided then and there that next time he would give in to his brother. He knew his mother was right. From now on he would try to please God by being more humble.

"Sit down here, near me," Lady Margaret motioned to the boys, pleased to see that both of them had realized their mistake. "You know the story of St. Paul the Apostle already. Would you like to hear about St. Stanislaus?"

"Yes," the boys said together. So Lady Margaret began telling the story she had heard as a child....

About five hundred years before you were born, Stanislaus, another baby was born into a very special family. His mother and father had been married a long time. In fact, after thirty years they still had no children. They loved each other very much, but they wanted a child in order to share their love.

For a long time they had prayed and begged God to send them a child. Then, after many years, although they were devout people and continued to pray, they no longer asked God for a child. They thought it was God's will for them to remain childless, and they wanted always to do God's will.

Then, after thirty years, God blessed them with a precious gift—a little son. They were both so happy! They had their son baptized and named him Stanislaus. They dedicated their only son to God and hoped and prayed that he might one day be a priest.

Stanislaus grew up just like any other little boy. I suppose he even argued sometimes the way you two do. He studied, he played, and he learned all about God. Even when he was very small he liked to pray. Whenever he felt lonely, or when he found something hard, he would talk to God about it. He loved to go to Mass and often wished he could become a priest.

When Stanislaus grew up, he did become a priest, just as his parents had hoped. He was a very good priest who tried to help the poor. Sometimes he visited sick people to comfort them and bring them the sacraments.

When he was 42 years old, Father Stanislaus was made a bishop. Now he had more people to care for and many big problems to solve. He still loved to pray, and even though he was now a bishop, he took all his difficulties to God, just as he had done when he was a little boy.

Ruling Poland at the time of Bishop Stanislaus was King Boleslaus. There has probably never been another king as wicked as King Boleslaus. In fact, he was so bad that everyone called him Boleslaus the Cruel. He had people killed and imprisoned just for disagreeing with him! He kidnapped people and put them in prison until their families would pay big sums of money to get them out. He stole property from poor people and whole castles from rich people.

Bishop Stanislaus kept hearing about all the terrible things King Boleslaus was doing. He became worried and disturbed because the king feared neither God nor man and was continually committing serious sins. The bishop knew that he was responsible for the king's soul. It was up to him to try to make the king repent and change his wicked life. But Bishop Stanislaus also knew that King Boleslaus could put him in prison or even kill him if he got angry.

"Lord, what shall I do?" the bishop prayed. "If I do nothing, many people will be hurt and the king may not save his soul. But if I scold him and try to make him change his life, he may get angry and throw me into prison."

After praying for a long time, Bishop Stanislaus decided to go see the king no matter what might happen. He knew it was his duty and God's will.

When told that the bishop wanted to see him, the king was curious.

"What can the bishop possibly want with me?" he wondered. He was even a little afraid, but he didn't want to show it.

"Bring in the bishop," he told his courtiers.

"My king," said the good bishop, making a low bow before him, "I come in the name of God. I come because you are putting your soul in danger by your evil life. God loves you. The Church loves you. Please tell God you are sorry, and start to live a life worthy of a great king."

To everyone's surprise, the king listened to the bishop. He asked to be left alone with him and they talked a long time. The king promised to change his ways and even thanked Bishop Stanislaus for coming. The bishop was so happy. When he got home he went straight to the chapel and thanked God for the grace of the king's conversion.

For a while it seemed as though the king was really trying to change. All the people began to hope that some of the good men the king had put in prison would be released. They thought that the king might give back the lands he had stolen.

Before long, however, everyone realized that the king was falling back into his evil ways again.

The whole kingdom was saddened at the king's new crimes. Many people asked the bishop to try again. Since his last visit had helped a little, Bishop Stanislaus agreed to go a second time.

This time Bishop Stanislaus was not so gentle. He told the king that offending God was very serious. God is a good Father, but He is also just. He will always forgive us if we are sorry, but He cannot forgive us if we refuse His mercy and refuse to change our evil ways. He even told the king that he would be excommunicated if he continued to do evil, then he would not have the grace of the Mass and the sacraments to help him.

King Boleslaus did not take this visit as well as the first. He flew into a rage and vowed he would take revenge. He had the bishop thrown out of the castle, telling him he would regret everything he had said.

Soon the king began to spread evil rumors about the bishop. He told everyone that the bishop had taken the property of a man named Peter, and had never paid for it. The man, Peter, had died, so the bishop had no way of proving that he had paid for the land. Many people believed the king, and they demanded that Bishop Stanislaus be tried in court.

This delighted the king. He knew that the bishop had no way to prove his innocence, so he could be found guilty and put in prison and no one could blame the king for being unjust.

On the day of the trial, the king himself, along with all the nobles, went to the courtroom.

"Bishop Stanislaus," said the judge, "you are accused of taking Peter's property and never paying for it. Is this true?"

"No, Your Honor, I paid Peter the price he asked, but he asked very little because he wanted to give the land for God's glory. He had hoped that a church could be built on the land and thus it would be dedicated to the worship of God."

"Can you prove this?"

"No, Your Honor," answered the bishop sadly. "Peter was the only witness and he is dead."

"If you cannot prove your innocence, and if there are no witnesses, I will have to find you guilty and sentence you to prison."

Bishop Stanislaus felt very sad. All his spiritual children would be left without their leader and father. He said a quick prayer and then said to the judge,

"Your Honor, there was one witness. God witnessed the entire transaction. Will you give me one hour to produce evidence that I am telling the truth?"

"Yes," answered the judge, "I will grant that. We will adjourn the court for one hour."

Bishop Stanislaus trusted in God. He and some priests went to Peter's tomb. The bishop asked the priests to remove the large marble covering to the tomb. They did not understand what the bishop was doing, but they obeyed.

When the cover was removed, the bishop spoke to the dead man.

"Peter, you loved truth and innocence when you were alive; you practiced charity and tried to do God's will. Now, in the name of God, I ask you to return to life and practice charity again. Arise to defend truth and innocence."

Peter came back to life! The priests were terrified. But the bishop remained calm; he knew that God had granted this special miracle to prove his innocence and to give the king another chance to repent.

The bishop took Peter to court. The judge, the king and all the nobles were shocked into silence. No one dared speak.

"Peter," said the bishop, "tell the court the truth about the land I acquired from you."

The dead man, now fully alive, began to talk. He said, "I gave the land to the bishop for a very small amount, which he paid. I wanted the land to be used for God's glory."

The judge was so stunned that he could hardly speak. The king turned pale and trembled. The nobles sat frozen in their seats.

The bishop led Peter out of the courtroom and back to his tomb. God had worked a tremendous miracle! Peter returned to eternity and the bishop returned to his home. All the false charges were dropped.

Again, for a while, the king seemed better. The miracle had been so stupendous that he could not ignore it. He had to admit that the bishop was a man of God. But, as time wore on, the miracle impressed him less and less. He became wicked once again.

The brave bishop fasted, prayed, and made many sacrifices, trying to obtain the king's conversion. Finally, a third time, he went and spoke with the king. This time the king became so angry that he threatened the bishop with death.

But saints never let anything, even the threat of death, stand in the way of doing what is right. A fourth time Bishop Stanislaus dared to go see the king. This time, when he left the palace, he knew his life was in danger.

The bishop knew that his home would no longer be safe, so he decided not to go there. Where could he go? He needed to go where he could be close to God. He took refuge in a small chapel and prayed for strength.

"My God," he prayed, "I want only to do Your will. If I must die, then at least I will die for love of Your name and for the truth. I forgive the king with all my heart. Since by my life I have not been able to obtain the king's conversion, grant that through my death, he may change his life and turn to You, the God and Father of all."

Before long, the king and his soldiers tracked down the bishop and found him in the little chapel. The king ordered the soldiers to kill the bishop, but the soldiers greatly admired this saintly man, and they refused. Three different groups of soldiers were sent. All three refused to lay a hand on the bishop.

When all else had failed, the king himself, blind with hatred and rage, rushed upon the good bishop and killed him with a sword. The martyred bishop blessed the king, even as he died and was welcomed into heaven by the angels.

King Boleslaus eventually repented for his horrible crimes, especially for murdering Bishop Stanislaus. He begged God's forgiveness and mercy. To show God he was truly sorry, he gave up his kingdom and went to live in a monastery in Hungary. He did penance for the rest of his life, often asking St. Stanislaus to help him from heaven. He died a holy death which made everyone praise God for His infinite goodness and mercy....

As Lady Margaret finished the story, Paul and Stanislaus sat very still. Their argument really seemed foolish and childish now. Stanislaus was proud of his name, but he knew that the great bishop would have been too humble to insist that it was the best name. It was best for him because it was the name God wanted him to have.

Paul looked at Stanislaus. He still liked his own name and was glad it was in the Bible, but now he felt proud to have a brother named after such a great saint. Who knew, maybe even Stanislaus would someday become a great saint.

CHAPTER 4

OFF TO SCHOOL

John Kostka was a nobleman and a senator, who had very high political ambitions for his sons, Paul and Stanislaus. He began to carry out his plan by sending the boys to the Jesuit college in Vienna to complete their education.

"Do you think we'll get to Vienna today?" Stanislaus asked. It was July 25, 1564. The teenage Stanislaus was traveling with Paul and their tutor, Dr. Bilinski, who had been their teacher at home in the castle.

"Oh, no," the tutor answered. "There's an inn not far from here where we'll spend the night. Then we'll arrive in Vienna at a decent hour tomorrow."

The three travelers continued on. Stanislaus was thinking about home, and he was already starting to miss everyone. But then he was glad that his father had decided to send him to a fine Jesuit school in Austria for his education.

But although he was deep in his own thoughts, he realized that Paul and Dr. Bilinski were quietly talking about something.

"We'll have to see what we can do to get away from him."

"I hope it won't be too hard to get off campus," Paul was saying. "I want to see what kind of excitement there is in Vienna."

"You're right. We'll have to see how we can get away," replied Dr. Bilinski, who was just as careless about his life as Paul was. "And we'll have to see what to do with *him*," he added, motioning with his head toward Stanislaus, who was following. "We can't risk having him mention anything in his letters home.

"Here's the inn," Dr. Bilinski announced. They approached the innkeeper, who greeted them very kindly because he could see they were noblemen. Ordinary travelers did not wear embroidered shirts and leather vests and breeches. They sat so erectly in the saddle,...and on such beautiful horses, too.

"Please have my horse rubbed down and well fed and watered," Stanislaus said as he slid out of the saddle. "And the others, too. Give them nice warm stalls with plenty of fresh hay, please."

"You must be very tired, traveling on this hot day. Come in and rest," said the man after he had turned the horses over to the stableboy.

"I hope you've got good food, good drink, and good beds," Dr. Bilinski loudly demanded.

"Oh, I think you'll find them to your liking, Sir," answered the innkeeper. "Right this way." And he showed them to their rooms.

Paul and the tutor threw themselves down on their beds for a nap. Stanislaus was restless, so he

"We need good food, good drink, and good beds,"
Dr. Bilinski demanded.

went down to help the innkeeper prepare supper and set the table.

"How old are you, son?" the man asked.

"I'm fourteen years old and my brother is almost sixteen. Our parents are sending us to study at the Jesuit college in Vienna. It's supposed to be a good school."

"Oh, it is," the innkeeper agreed. "The Jesuits are all good teachers and holy priests. I'm sure you will like it."

That comment made Stanislaus feel a little more relaxed, since he was also wondering what Paul and Bilinski had in mind.

"Well," he said, "that's good. I'll be able to learn a lot and grow closer to God, too."

After a good evening meal and a restful night's sleep, the travelers started out again early the next morning. Both boys chattered away with excitement. Today they would see their new school. Stanislaus wondered what strange new things he would be taking up in class and Paul was anticipating great adventures with new, more exciting companions. Bilinski was a good fellow, but a bit too old for some things!

Chapter 5

A PEACEFUL START

The bright sun gleamed on the stained-glass windows of the tall, large stone buildings facing the three travelers. They had just ridden down the road lined with trees that led to the main buildings of the Jesuit college. The priest in charge of the college gave them a warm welcome.

"Well, the Kostka boys have arrived! We've been waiting for you, and we're very happy to have you. Welcome, Dr. Bilinski. We hope you will also enjoy your stay here. Please, let me show you around the campus."

He took them around the grounds—wide lawns, beautifully planted with flowers and trees. They stopped in to pay a visit at the college chapel and then went to a large boarding house on the campus. The house had been given to the Jesuits by Emperor Ferdinand I. This made it possible for the students to live right at the college.

"Everything is beautiful, isn't it?" Stanislaus commented.

"It's okay," Paul answered. His mind was not so much on his studies just then, but they were to start soon, and Stanislaus was eager for them to begin.

The subjects were not easy, but Stanislaus paid attention and worked as hard as he could. He prayed, too:

"Please, Jesus, You know all things. Help me to study well, and to learn these lessons so that I can be a better person and a better Christian—so I can serve You better and help other people, too."

Sometimes he studied so late that he fell asleep with his head on his textbooks. Once the first hard work had been done, it became a little easier. He did not have to stay up so late, but he did some advanced studying, and some good reading and praying.

"Why are you always such a goody-goody?" Paul taunted. "You're always trying to show me up."

"That's not true," Stanislaus replied. "I just don't want to waste time because our parents are paying so much to send us to this school. Besides, Paul, you don't have a hard time learning and I do."

"I don't believe you. I'll get even somehow."

Paul was particularly upset because he had earned another bad conduct mark on his report card, which had greatly displeased his parents. They had written to Dr. Bilinski, but since Bilinski was just as unruly as Paul, it did not do much good.

Stanislaus prayed very much for his brother.

Then—abruptly—Stanislaus' serene life at the college ended. They had been there only eight months when Emperor Ferdinand died. His son

"Why are you always such a goody-goody?
You're always trying to show me up!"

Maximillian then became Emperor, and he took the boarding house away from the Jesuits.

Everything and everyone was upset. Where would all the students go? The priests offered them rooms in the homes of their relatives. Many accepted, but Paul and Bilinski used this chance to move in with a man who was an enemy of religion.

Stanislaus begged his brother and the tutor to look for another place.

"Isn't there somewhere else we can live?" he pleaded. But he did not have much say in the final decision. So...Stanislaus prayed for light and strength for the hard days that he knew were coming.

Stanislaus continued to concentrate on his schoolwork. "I don't think I'll ever be good at writing Latin speeches," he thought to himself. It was a lot easier now than it had been in the beginning, but how many times he wished he could just write in Polish.

"An educated nobleman must be able to read and write Latin and Greek as well as his own language," his professor had reminded the students more than once. Paul never seemed to take this too seriously. He would scribble off his homework in an amazingly short time. After supper he was free to "have fun."

Stanislaus would finish his homework after supper and then find a quiet corner in the house to pray. Sometimes Paul would come by and a battle would begin.

"God doesn't expect you to stay on your knees all day like a common beggar. You're disgracing the family name by refusing to go to dances and parties. You don't even act like the son of a nobleman! Aren't you ashamed? Passing yourself off to be holy when it's nothing but stubbornness!" Paul would follow up his shouting with a kick or a punch.

Stanislaus would remain silent, but his feelings were far from silent. His face would turn red, and his hands would clench into fists, while his blood cried out for revenge. His first reaction was to get even with Paul—to fight back and defend himself. But then he would think of Jesus.

"Jesus was kicked and beaten and crucified. He didn't try to get even. He didn't even get angry. He forgave everyone," he would tell himself. Then as Paul would storm out of the room and slam the door, Stanislaus would pray for his angry brother. He knew that the parties Paul went to were anything but Christian. There was drinking and much gambling. Stanislaus wanted no part of it.

Little by little it became almost impossible to pray or read a holy book without getting into trouble with Paul. Then Stanislaus found a new way. At night he would wait until everyone was asleep, then he would light his candle and read and pray in the quiet stillness. The steady breathing of his several sleeping roommates made a background for his prayers.

One night was darker than usual. The moon was somewhere behind a heavy blanket of clouds. One of the sleeping boys turned uneasily in bed. He felt strangely awake but could not understand what had awakened him. The dormitory seemed foggy. He found it hard to breathe. Suddenly the truth burst upon him as he began coughing.

"Fire! Fire!" he shouted, now fully awake. At the end of the room he could see flames through the smoke.

"Stanislaus!" he yelled as everyone began leaping out of bed. "Stanislaus' bed is on fire!"

Stanislaus awoke in a confusion of noise, smoke and flames. In one movement he jerked off the covers and jumped clear from the burning bed. Coughing and watery-eyed, the boys began to beat the flames and stamp out the burning bedcovers. As the flames died out, the frightened boys stood and looked at the blackened pillow, mattress and bed frame. Stanislaus had not been burned.

"What's this?" asked Paul when he had calmed down. He picked up a candlestick that had fallen near the bed. The candle had burned down to its base. No one spoke.

Stanislaus was shocked into silence. He must have fallen asleep, and when the candle had burned down it had set the pillow on fire. Paul looked at him as the full truth began to form in his mind.

"Is that what your prayers and so-called holiness are supposed to accomplish?" raged Paul.

"Does God want you to burn the house down on top of us? This nonsense has got to stop!"

Now how could he ever make Paul understand? Stanislaus had to admit that reading in bed by candlelight had been a mistake. God had really saved them despite his foolish imprudence. But would Paul never see that prayer was everything to him? His hours in the college chapel and his treasured times for prayer meant more to him than any earthly honor. He was the son of a nobleman, but first of all he was a child of God.

CHAPTER 6

HARDSHIP REWARDED

The life that Paul and Bilinski were leading grew worse by the week, and so did their treatment of Stanislaus. Their teasing and jokes turned into threats.

"Look, if you keep acting so pious, you're going to be sorry. A few beatings will take care of you."

Stanislaus was not a coward, but he knew he would need strength from God. He joined a prayer group called the Congregation of St. Barbara. He was already used to making sacrifices, such as choosing to eat something he didn't really like or doing a favor for someone when it was inconvenient. Now he began to make many more, in order to obtain God's help.

Soon the threats became a reality. Paul and Bilinski actually started beating Stanislaus. He did not fight back, not even with words. He did not even write to his parents about it.

He remained very kind to Paul all the time. When he had been beaten, he would pray: "Jesus, I offer this little suffering to You, so that You will make Paul change his ways."

After nearly two years, Stanislaus' health could not take the abuse and neglect, so he became very ill.

Two angels were bringing Stanislaus Holy Communion.

"I think I'm dying," he told his brother and the tutor. "Please call a priest for me."

But when they had moved in, the owner of the house had warned: "Just be sure of this—I will never let a priest into my house!"

So in answer to Stanislaus' request, Paul impatiently told him it was impossible. "You know what the landlord said. He doesn't want any priests on his property. Forget it."

Then Paul left, and Stanislaus lay there in deep sorrow. But he had great hope in God and in the Blessed Mother.

"O Jesus and Mary, helpers of the dying, please assist me. I know you won't abandon me. St. Barbara, please help me."

Then, something very wonderful happened.

It was Christmas Eve, and Stanislaus could hear all the noise of music and laughter going on outside. He was lying quietly in bed, and the candle was giving the room a soft glow. Suddenly, Saint Barbara appeared with two angels. They were bringing Stanislaus Holy Communion! What a great joy filled his heart! He received Jesus and was all taken up in his prayers of thanksgiving when suddenly in another vision the Blessed Mother was standing in front of him. She looked so beautiful and loving! She was holding Baby Jesus. She came near Stanislaus and put the Baby in his arms. He held Him close, and he could feel something going through his whole body. Then Mary spoke:

She came near Stanislaus and put the Baby in his arms.

"You will be cured, Stanislaus. When you are well, you must enter the Jesuits. This is God's will for you."

She took Baby Jesus and they both disappeared. Stanislaus was lying in bed, perfectly healthy, and so happy and excited! For a long while he had wanted to join the Jesuits, and this was the sign of God's approval.

Paul and Bilinski could not believe their eyes the next morning.

"I'm well! I'm cured! Let's go to Mass and thank God."

Their great surprise and Stanislaus' excitement actually convinced his brother and tutor to go to Mass with him that day.

Now Stanislaus would have to see how to carry out his desire and God's will. For the rest of the winter and spring, he studied hard and prayed hard. He waited to see whether something more would happen to indicate to him what he should do next. But nothing unusual took place; no visions or heavenly messengers appeared.

"I wonder if God wants me to be brave enough to do this on my own?" he mused. "He has already given me His approval—what more do I want?" He made a hesitant decision. "I'll do it the next time I go by the rectory. I'll go right in and say, 'Here I am,' and the Fathers will do the rest."

But Stanislaus still did not take the first step. He found one excuse after another, even though the desire to be a Jesuit was becoming unbearable.

"I'm not worthy to join those holy men," he would try to convince himself. "How often I still feel resentful and angry at Paul! How often I still think unkindly of Dr. Bilinski when he joins Paul in all those parties instead of making him behave!"

One day as he was kneeling in prayer in the college chapel a new idea came to his mind. His conscience seemed to tell him very clearly: "All your excuses for not following God's call to be a Jesuit are nothing but cowardice! You are not generous enough to live a life of service to God."

The idea startled him and he at once tried to deny it. But deep down he knew it was true. He couldn't get the thought out of his mind.

"Jesus, give me the strength and courage to do what You want me to do," he prayed. He knew what he had to do. His father would be angry, he was sure of that, but God's will had to come first. Maybe he could make his father understand better than Paul would.

CHAPTER 7

THE GREAT DECISION

The air was quiet and still. It was a free day from school, and Stanislaus had gone to the campus to do some reading and to have some time to think and pray.

As he was walking he suddenly turned with determination and strode up to the door of the Jesuit residence. He asked to speak to the Superior.

"May I please be admitted to the Jesuits, Father?" he humbly requested.

To his shocked surprise the answer was: "Oh, my son, I'm afraid your father would be terribly upset. He has such high ambitions for you in politics. And he is so powerful. If we admit you and he becomes angry...."

Stanislaus knew what Father meant. But now he had made up his mind.

He left the building and was walking down the road when he met a very holy, old Jesuit whom he knew. He revealed his problem to him.

"You see, Father," he confided, "it isn't only what *I* want, but the Blessed Mother has told me that it is *God's* will and desire, too. I can't keep God waiting."

The gentle eyes of the old Jésuit looked into those of Stanislaus—bright with fire and resolve. The elderly priest thought for a few minutes. Finally, he said: "Why don't you go to Augsburg, Germany, and ask to be admitted there? And if even they refuse you, go on further, and ask the Superior General in Rome, Father Francis Borgia."

"How far is Augsburg?" Stanislaus asked.

"Only three hundred fifty miles," the old Jesuit replied.

Stanislaus' heart started to beat quickly at the idea. Three hundred fifty miles! Could he make it on foot? The weather should be good. It was nearly summer.

"Why should I worry about my health?" he thought. "If Mary and St. Barbara came to assist me and cure me, they will certainly help me to carry out God's will. Yes, I'll go."

Even though he had not said anything openly to Paul and Bilinski, they had noticed the growth of his devotion and prayers ever since he had been cured. Once, a long time before, he had told his brother about his desire to be a Jesuit, but Paul had sharply answered: "You'd better forget that idea. Father would be furious, and who knows what he would do!"

There was no way that Stanislaus could bring up the subject again. He was on his own, but he was not alone. He had Jesus, Mary, his angel and Saint Barbara to help him.

Now his plans began to take shape. He would have to choose a time when he would not be missed for a while. The thought of running away was frightening. "What if they catch up with me?" he wondered. "Certainly Paul would take me back to Poland at once. I would be treated almost as a criminal. Father would never trust me again."

Sometimes his thoughts would almost make him change his mind. Then he would remember that the Blessed Mother herself had told him it was God's will.

One night when Dr. Bilinski and Paul were out at a party, Stanislaus was working on a special letter. He was doing his best to write a note explaining why he was leaving and where he was going. He found it very difficult to explain how he felt. After several attempts he finally succeeded in finishing the letter. He hid it in a place where it wouldn't be found until after he was well on his way.

Stanislaus wasn't at all sleepy, so he knelt down and began to talk things over with God. He soon lost all idea of time as he knelt on the edge of eternity. He was no longer afraid. New courage flooded his heart and he could hardly wait until morning.

"Stanislaus!" The anger in Paul's voice startled him back into reality. Paul had caught him at prayer. He stood up just in time to receive Paul's fist in his face. He fell to the floor and didn't even try to ward off the blows and kicks.

"If I ever decided to leave here, Paul, you would have a lot of explaining to do to Father."

"Are you threatening me? There's nothing I'd like better than for you to leave. I wish you'd get out of my sight for good!" shouted Paul as he stomped out of the room.

"Well," thought Stanislaus as he splashed cold water on his sore face, "now I have his permission to leave. God has really arranged everything."

Early the next morning Stanislaus climbed out of bed and dressed quickly. He went to the kitchen and put some bread, cheese and fruit into a bag. No one in the house was up yet. He let himself out the front door and quietly closed it behind him. He went to church for an early Mass and then started on his way.

As he reached the end of the street he couldn't resist stopping and looking back. There was no one in the sleeping town to wish him a good journey. "May God go with me," he said aloud since there was no one else to give the traditional blessing before beginning a trip.

"I wonder how long it will be before I see Paul again. I hope Mother won't be too worried." This last thought made him sad, but he knew he was doing the only thing possible to follow his vocation.

CHAPTER 8

ON THE WAY

Since Paul and his tutor did not pay much attention to him, it had not been too hard for Stanislaus to slip away unnoticed. At the edge of town he exchanged his clothes with those of a beggar, and started on his journey to Augsburg.

"When is Stanislaus coming home?" the tutor asked Paul the next day.

"Well, don't *you* know where he is, Bilinski?"

"Now, Paul, you know you should watch him just as much as I should!"

They soon suspected what had happened. Paul took a search party and set out to find Stanislaus. Before long they saw a beggar at the side of the road.

"Did you see a young nobleman going along here?" they shouted.

"Not since I've been here," the beggar answered, shrugging his shoulders and pulling down his hat to shade his eyes from the sun.

The horsemen rode off in a cloud of dust that made Stanislaus look even more like a beggar. The grace of God and Stanislaus' disguise had saved him from his pursuers. Now he could continue his

"Now, Paul! You should watch him just as much as I should!"

journey in peace. He studied the map the old priest had drawn for him. He knew he would have to keep a sharp lookout for the landmarks the old man had told him about and indicated on his crudely-drawn map. They had spent hours over the piece of parchment—the old man's knotty finger tracing over the trails, his quivering voice warning of pitfalls, wild boars, bears, wolves! The eager boy had shivered with fright, anticipation, and delight at the old man's reminiscences.

"Ah, my boy, what a wonderful adventure you are about to set out on. If only I were fifty years younger! What great times we'd have together! I'd do it all over again in a minute. God go with you, son. You will have my prayers every step of the way." The old priest's eyes had filled with tears, but his smile had been radiant.

A lump formed in Stanislaus' throat as he remembered his old friend. "I sure wish you *were* fifty years younger, Father," he whispered, "or even ten. I could use a friend right now. This is the first time I've ever been alone—it feels kind of spooky."

After walking for several days, Stanislaus found himself in the middle of a forest. The sun was low in the sky and he hoped to be out of the forest by the time it got dark. On one side of the path were rocky cliffs, on the other, dense underbrush and trees.

He walked a little faster and began to feel uneasy as the sun set behind the cliffs. All the other nights he had found shelter in the barns of friendly farmers. They had always given him breakfast and their good wives had refilled his bag with bread, cheese and fruit. These people were poor, but kind and generous to those who were even less fortunate.

Finally Stanislaus had to admit that he would have to spend the night in the woods. All the stories he had ever heard about bears and wolves came to his mind against his will. He began to look around for a good place to settle down for the night. Through the dim light he could see what looked like a cave about halfway up the cliff.

"Now I'll find out how good a climber I am," he said aloud, glad to hear a human voice even if it was his own. He scrambled up the cliff and reached the cave just as it became really dark. Remembering that bears often live in caves, he was afraid to go in.

"After that climb I certainly don't intend to stand out here all night," he reminded himself. Then he picked up a rock, took courage, and threw the rock into the cave. He heard it hit the wall and fall to the floor. There was no other sound—no angry growl.

"I guess I'm a better climber than the bears! The cave is mine after all."

It was very small inside; hardly even big enough for him to stretch out his aching legs. But Stanislaus was grateful for this shelter and it seemed better to him than a great castle. He was

"Did you see a young nobleman go by?"

hungry and a little cold, but he knelt and thanked
God for bringing him so far.

Stanislaus prayed a long time and finally fell
asleep. His tired body needed rest. When he
awoke the sun was already up and shedding a
delicious warmth on everything. The birds were
singing their morning melodies and a friendly
spider had just completed a perfect new web.

Stanislaus smiled. "So little friend, you shared
my home with me last night. Or maybe I shared
your home with you. But I'm going to leave you
soon. You praise your Creator by your perfect web.
I am going to praise Him with my life!"

He carefully walked around the web and
stepped into the new day. The difficult descent
down the cliff made him wonder how he had ever
managed to climb up. Somehow he slipped and
slid and climbed down and once more set out on
the forest path. Every step was a prayer. Every
mile covered was one less obstacle to his vocation.

Sometimes the trudging along became harder
and harder. Some days his loneliness weighed him
down with homesickness. His feelings were as
changeable as the scenery he passed. One day he
would feel so close to God that heaven itself
seemed to fill his heart. On other days God
seemed far away and the road seemed long, the
pebbles got in his shoes, the rain soaked him and
all the mosquitoes in the world seemed to find
him. Sometimes the farmers weren't so friendly
and he had to go hungry for a while.

He said his rosary while his feet moved automatically up one hill and down another. And all the while, in the back of his mind was a little voice that said: "What if they don't accept you? Then what will you do? Where will you go then?" He would force himself to make an act of faith and once more place himself in the care of his heavenly Mother.

The pebbles got in his shoes.

CHAPTER 9

HALFWAY TO THE GOAL

Three hundred fifty miles is a long way to walk by yourself. Stanislaus rested in the little villages along the way, but he never stayed too long because everyone noticed when there was a stranger in town and started to ask questions.

Finally the day came when he saw an old sign that said, "Augsburg—20 miles." Stanislaus breathed a sigh of relief and joy. Since it was already dusk, he started looking for a shelter for the night. He spotted a place on the side of the hill completely surrounded by shady trees. He climbed up to it and sat down on the rocks.

It was a mild, clear night. He could smell the moss, the forest flowers, and the pine trees.

"Please share this meal with me, Jesus, Mary, and St. Barbara," he said aloud. They had been his only companions for the whole trip, and they had taken good care of him.

Stanislaus shared his breakfast with the birds and
squirrels.

As it grew darker, Stanislaus looked up at the beautiful stars in the sky. His excited thoughts turned into prayers. His great dream was about to come true. Tomorrow he would be at the Jesuit house of Augsburg.

"I wonder what Mother and Father are thinking," he pondered. "I hope they are not too worried, but they will find out one day. Meanwhile, God is watching over them, as He is watching over me."

Then he said his night prayers and went peacefully to sleep.

The chirping birds woke him early—right after dawn. He opened his bag and threw out some crumbs of bread for them to eat, and then, after saying his prayers, he had his own breakfast. The big day had arrived, and he was happy to get an early start.

It was almost noon when Stanislaus rang the bell at the gate of the college. Father Doorkeeper looked surprised when he saw the ragged boy.

"Who are you, lad? Where do you come from?"

"I'm Stanislaus Kostka, and I have come from Vienna to ask admission to the Society of Jesus."

"Well, come in, my boy. You must be very tired and very hungry."

After listening to Stanislaus' excited account of his visions and his travels, the priests told him, "You must rest a bit, and then go on to Dillingen to talk to Father Canisius."

The weary traveler slept peacefully that night with a comfortable full feeling in his stomach and a warm blanket snug around him. Early the next morning he set out again with the blessings of his new friends.

It was one of those great moments in history when two saints meet each other. Stanislaus heard a kind voice saying, "Welcome, my son," and looked up to see a priest standing in the doorway, his hand stretched out to greet him.

"I am Father Peter Canisius, and I hear you have come a long way. Why don't we talk while we have something to eat?"

Stanislaus followed Father Canisius to a room down the hall where a table had been set for two. In a few minutes a brother came in with dinner for both of them.

"Why don't you tell me the whole story?" Father asked.

He was so kind that Stanislaus told him everything, starting with his childhood desires to do something special for God. At the end, Father said, "Very good, my son. Now we'll pray over it together for a few days and see what God's will is."

Father Canisius was not as afraid of Stanislaus' father as the priests in Vienna had been, but he knew that Dillingen was still too close to Poland for Stanislaus to remain there. He also wanted to test him to see if he was really determined in his decision. So after a few days, he told Stanislaus, "I think it would be better for you to enter in our General House in Rome, but since you have had such a long and tiring journey, you will stay here for

"I'm Stanislaus Kostka.
I've come from Vienna to join the Society of Jesus."

a few weeks. After you build up your strength, you may go to Rome."

"Oh, thank you, Father Canisius!" the boy exclaimed. Rome was over a thousand miles away, but at least he had not been turned down.

He spent three weeks in Dillingen serving at table and working in the kitchen. Everyone was amazed at how simple this nobleman's son was and how humbly he went about his duties.

"Why don't you just tell me the whole story,"
Fr. Peter Canisius said.

CHAPTER 10

THE THOUSAND-MILE HIKE

After Stanislaus' rest period, Father Canisius sent him with two companions to Rome to see Father Francis Borgia. Carrying stout climbing staffs, the three spent the whole summer on that wonderful pilgrimage.

They were a lighthearted group starting out from Dillingen that first morning. This time Stanislaus did not have to watch for blazed trees, rock formations or other such trail indicators. The oldest member of the group, a Jesuit priest, even older than Dr. Bilinski had been, had gone over the trail several times. Stanislaus' other new friend was not much older than himself. He was not yet ordained.

"Take it easy, boys; you're springing along like a pair of jack rabbits. Pace yourselves. You'll find you won't wake up in the night with charley horses if you go at an even, steady clip," the priest advised.

Stanislaus understood the wisdom of that. What pain he had suffered the first few nights on his walk from Vienna! He was glad his friends didn't know how he had cried himself to sleep those first few nights. Not only had he been frightened, but he had suffered terrible leg cramps because his mus-

"Take it easy, boys;
you're springing along like a pair of jack rabbits."

cles had been soft and underdeveloped. But with
the miles of trudging uphill and down, climbing and
scrambling over rocks, his legs and back and even
his shoulders and arms had firmed up. He had
grown so much that the ragged shirt he had traded
his beautiful suit for would no longer go around
him. He wiggled his shoulders in the habit the
Jesuits had allowed him to wear. It felt as comfortable as his own skin. "It was made for me," he
thought.

At the end of the first week they were following
a tributary of the Elba River as it wound through
the trees and between mountains. The priest said,
"This may seem a bit out of the way, I know. Crows
can fly over mountains, but we would just bark our
shins and crack our backs climbing. So we make
better time going around."

As they rounded a heap of fallen rocks, they
were met by a group of travelers, accompanied by
several knights, coming down a converging trail.

"Where are ye headed for, my good Fathers,...
if ye *are* good Fathers. But if ye are but bandits
disguised as such, thinking to pull any fancy trick on
this company, ye'll find we'll crack your dirty,
thieving skulls just for the fun of it," said the biggest
knight.

"Heaven help us, my son," said the priest.
"There's no need going to all that trouble. We are
just as we appear to be, poor religious on the holy
pilgrimage to Rome."

"Well, Father," the knight said, "ye'd better accept our protection as well as heaven's. The forests in this section of the world house many ruthless bands who prey on just such as ye."

"Thank you, my son; we will gladly accept your offer."

The two groups continued together until they had left the danger zone behind.

After they left the Elba, the little group of friends followed the Danube, but not for long, much to Stanislaus' relief. He did not want to pass too close to Vienna and run the risk of being seen by anyone who would recognize him.

"Not yet," he told his two friends. "I'll write to my parents from Rome. I miss my mother and I'm sorry to worry her, but I know how happy she will be for me when she learns I am a Jesuit."

Very often the worried boy would ask his guardian angel to go to his mother and comfort her.

As the days went by, Stanislaus received many hours of instruction in Church history, theology, and especially the Rule of the Society of Jesus. Many times a day he repeated, with the others or by himself, the little prayer that St. Ignatius loved:

"Soul of Christ, sanctify me.
Body of Christ, save me.
Blood of Christ, inebriate me.
Water from the side of Christ, wash me.
Passion of Christ, strengthen me.

Oh, good Jesus, hear me.
Within Your wounds hide me.
Suffer me not to be separated from You.
From the evil one defend me.
At the hour of my death call me to come to
    You,
That with Your saints I may praise You,
For ever and ever. Amen."

After the little band of weary travelers had been sheltered a few times by the lowly people of villages and farms, Stanislaus began to realize how privileged he and his family had always been. What conditions the poor lived under, and yet they felt lucky just to have a dry place to sleep...sometimes on hay or leaves stuffed in rough sacks! Now and then the travelers were offered the family treasure—a feather bed to sleep on. And over their objections the family would sleep on the floor.

When they came into populated areas, the priest nearly always had a long line of penitents to confess or babies to baptize; there were also marriages to perform, and now and then a funeral. Many areas they passed through had not seen a priest for years.

Often when Stanislaus saw how much work there was to be done for the Lord, he was moved to pray another beautiful prayer that St. Ignatius had written:

"Take, O Lord, and receive my entire liberty, my memory, my understanding and my whole will.

"Well, boys, it won't be long now.
You've really become seasoned hikers."

All that I am and all that I possess You have given me; I surrender it all to You to be disposed of according to Your will. Give me only Your love and Your grace; with these I will be rich enough, and will desire nothing more."

Long days of toiling over rugged alps, with breathtaking views of snow-covered peaks, of stunningly beautiful sunrises and sunsets, were followed by long descents into more even terrain. How hot the weather became! One day at noon the priest announced, "Well, boys, it won't be long now. You've really become seasoned hikers. I'm proud of both of you."

It had been a long, long hike and Stanislaus had enjoyed it. He had grown to love the continual companionship of holy friends who shared his feelings so closely. One evening he was walking along thinking about this when he suddenly realized that the younger of his two companions was saying: "Hey, sleepy head, did you hear that? We should get there sometime tomorrow!"

CHAPTER 11

HIS DREAM COME TRUE

"Father Francis, there is a young man here asking for you. He has just arrived from Dillingen, and he has a letter from Father Canisius."

It was October 25, 1567. Stanislaus was seventeen years old. He had walked the 1,280 miles from Dillingen to Rome, the Eternal City, and this time his journey was really over. He was sitting in the parlor, exhausted but overjoyed, anxiously waiting for the Superior General, another great saint of the Society of Jesus, Father Francis Borgia. His thoughts were soon interrupted and he heard: "My son, you've come a long way to do God's will." He jumped up, and Father Francis warmly embraced him.

"Father, I am seeking admission into the Society of Jesus," Stanislaus said humbly.

"And the Society of Jesus will accept you," Father Borgia replied.

When Stanislaus heard those words, his whole body, tired as it was, seemed to feel the joy that filled his heart.

Father Borgia sent him to rest. On the way he stopped in the chapel to offer a prayer of gratitude to God and the Blessed Mother for having helped him reach his goal.

There was not such peace and joy in the Kostka home, however. Paul and Bilinski had returned from school. All the way home they had been trying to decide how to tell Mr. Kostka the story, for they knew that Stanislaus had run away to join the Jesuits.

"That boy is a disgrace to himself and to our family!" the father shouted. "I'll never let another Jesuit into Poland!"

He raged on and on. Then he wrote a very severe letter, telling Stanislaus that he was not following a profession worthy of a nobleman's son, and that he was being foolish and stupid to give up the great worldly position he could have as the son of John Kostka.

"My poor father," Stanislaus murmured as he slowly read the letter. "And not a word from my dear mother, but she is certainly praying for all of us."

Then he wrote his family a very tender and loving, but firm letter telling them that he was now in the service of the greatest Nobleman, the King of kings, and that no position on earth could be any higher or more lasting. He assured them that he was very happy and...that he would stay with the Jesuits.

"So, he's going to stay, is he?" Stanislaus' letter had only made his father's anger worse. "Paul," John Kostka shouted, "you must go to Rome and force Stanislaus to come home. I want all this nonsense to stop!"

"Paul! Go to Rome and force Stanislaus to come home!"

Meanwhile, in the Jesuit college at Rome, Stanislaus performed all his duties cheerfully and well. He was always smiling and friendly. Everyone enjoyed being with him because he was so good. Anyone who needed a favor could always count on Stanislaus for help, which he gave cheerfully and generously.

ALL FOR GOD

Stanislaus began his novitiate with a great surge of joy and enthusiasm. The novitiate would last two years. During that time the novices studied the Jesuit rule. They learned all about the vows they would take later on.

The novices lived apart from the other priests and brothers. They prayed together, ate together, worked together, and played together. Sometimes Stanislaus worked in the garden pulling weeds.

"You see, Stanislaus," Father Alphonse told him one day, "our bad habits are like these weeds. If we pull them up and get rid of them while they are still tiny, it's not too hard. If we wait until they are full grown, it would take two of us to pull them up."

"We have to get at the roots, too," added Stanislaus to show he understood. "If we leave the roots, the weeds grow back right away. I guess we have to get at the roots of our bad habits if we want to get rid of them, too."

"Always try to make your soul a clean, well-tended garden where beautiful flowers of virtue can grow: roses of charity, violets of humility, daisies of obedience, and many others as well. Pray very much and God will water your soul's garden with His grace so that the flowers of virtue will grow strong."

Father Alphonse finished his little lesson and moved to another row to weed. Stanislaus was busy pulling weeds and asking God to be his Gardener. He seemed so full of defects and sins. How did he deserve to be among all these holy men? How could he ever thank God enough for getting him through every obstacle?

Sometimes Stanislaus worked in the chapel. This was his favorite place to work. Imagine cleaning house for God! Isn't that exactly what Mary had done? He would polish the gold vessels until they shone like the most brilliant stars. He would sweep the floor and do the dusting as if the Blessed Mother herself were doing it. He would arrange the Mass vestments as if Jesus Himself were going to put them on.

All the while he would talk to Jesus in the Tabernacle. He could never quite get used to the idea that he lived under the same roof as his Lord and Master. Could any joy equal this? Then he would remember how the Blessed Mother had let him hold the Baby Jesus. He longed to be with Jesus again as he had been then. The desire was overwhelming and his heart would pound as if he was running a race. At times he would have to leave chapel and catch his breath. He was so close to heaven and yet so far away!

Sometimes Stanislaus worked in the kitchen. He liked Brother Cook. He was a good-natured, jolly man who had a good word and a smile for everyone. He laughed easily and everyone laughed with him. He always seemed busy about something and was forever saying that he was behind schedule. No one had ever been able to figure out how he managed to have all the meals ready on time.

Brother Cook liked to tell stories. He would stir the soup or peel potatoes and recall the time when....

One day he was short of help in the kitchen. Dinner time was getting nearer and he wasn't ready—as usual. There was a huge pot of stew that needed to cook a little longer It was too big for him to handle alone. He opened the kitchen door and saw a fellow Jesuit walking down the hall.

"Father," he called, "could you please help me a minute?"

He turned back into the kitchen, knowing that the priest would be right in. He had his back to the door when he heard it open.

"We just have to lift this pot onto that hook over the fire. Be careful not to burn yourself. I don't know how I would explain that to Father General."

They worked as he talked and got the big pot of stew over the fire. As he finally looked up for the first time to thank the priest, he stood there surprised and embarrassed: it was Father Francis

Borgia himself, the Father General. He was smiling and was immensely pleased that finally he had been allowed to help in the kitchen!

Brother Cook's stories always left Stanislaus feeling proud to belong to the Jesuits. If only he could have known Ignatius Loyola, their saintly founder! He, too, had been of noble birth and he had had to overcome many difficulties to begin the Society of Jesus. Brother Cook had told Stanislaus the story several times, each time adding different details and new insights.

Ignatius had been a captain in the king's army. He was a good man, but was also proud and rather arrogant. He knew he was a good soldier. He dressed as befitted a noble and rode a splendid horse.

One day Ignatius Loyola was badly wounded in a battle. His bravery was so well known and respected that the enemy carried the wounded man back to his home. There in the castle he spent many months of restless inactivity while his leg healed. In desperation he asked for some novels to read. His sister-in-law brought him the life of Christ and the lives of the saints instead.

A change gradually came over Ignatius as he read. He began to see that it was far better to serve the King of heaven than any earthly ruler. He renounced his title and possessions and gave himself completely to God. He became a priest and founded the Society of Jesus. Soon all of Europe was full of Jesuits. Jesuits went to the

Orient to preach about Christ. Jesuit missionaries went to the New World across the great ocean. Jesuits arrived in England to try to stem the tide of religious error.

Ignatius of Loyola and Francis Borgia had written many letters to each other. Father Ignatius had guided Francis in the renouncing of his many titles. Francis had been next in position to the king. Eleonor, his loving and beautiful wife, had taken care of the queen. God had blessed their happy marriage with eight children.

Francis Borgia's married years had been full of many joys, but also many worries of state, problems of war and tense diplomatic missions. Francis had grown closer to God year after year, despite his extreme activity. Because of his high position there was always jealousy on the part of those who envied him. There were even plots to get rid of him. But in true Christian charity he forgave anyone who tried to do him harm and never harbored resentment or desires for revenge.

When his holy wife died he knew the time had come for him to give up life in the world and give himself totally to God. He took care of the future of each of his children and made sure that each was well provided for. Then, with a deep sense of gratitude to God, he joined the Jesuits. When he was ordained a priest he felt he had received more joy than any man on earth had a right to.

Once Father Francis went out begging. A generous farmer gave him a pig. Father was delighted because food was scarce and the pig would provide many pounds of pork for the priests, brothers and students. He thanked the farmer, gave him his blessing, and started for home.

The noble Francis Borgia, now a priest with no worldly titles or possessions, had not the faintest idea about how to get a pig home. He had never had to take care of animals or work on a farm. He had always had servants for that.

"Come now, my fine friend," he said to the pig as he began to pull the rope tied around the pig's neck. "Be a nice, obedient pig and we will get along fine."

But the pig refused to move. Father Francis pulled harder. The pig simply stared at him and lay down! Father got behind and tried to push him up. It was no use! "He must know he is headed for the oven," thought the puzzled priest.

"Is something wrong, Father?" the farmer asked as he came over to the gate.

"This pig refuses to cooperate," said Father Francis, very much disturbed with such stubbornness. "What good is a pig if you can't get him to market?"

"Just wait here, Father, and I'll be right back," said the smiling farmer as he headed toward his barn. He returned a moment later with a carrot tied to the end of a stick. He dangled it in front of the pig's nose and, to Father's amazement, the pig immediately got up.

"Just walk with this carrot in front of the pig and he will follow you all the way to town," instructed the farmer.

Father could hardly believe what a change had come over the animal. The pig apparently thought that each step brought him closer to that delicious carrot.

"Imagine," thought Father Francis, "I can sway an audience of a thousand people with a fine sermon on the love of God, but it took a simple farmer to show me how to move a pig! Well, my good Francis," he told himself, "the next time you are tempted to pride, just remember that you do not even know enough to move a pig!"

When he got home, his fellow Jesuits had a good laugh at the sight of the great Francis Borgia leading a pig with a carrot on a stick. The pig was rewarded with the carrot, and Father Francis went to chapel to talk things over with the Lord.

Stanislaus was laughing when he left the kitchen. He knew it was a good story to teach him a lesson as well. He was a noble's son, but there was no task too humble for a Jesuit. Great in learning, they had to be even greater in humility. It was not education that would bring them holiness, but their love of God and His children, and their willingness to obey His will at every moment of their lives.

When Stanislaus wasn't singing aloud, his happy heart was singing great hymns to God and His Blessed Mother. All those who came in contact with him felt his holiness. He was a joy to have around!

For Stanislaus, the best part of his new life was having so much time to pray. His devotion to Jesus and Mary grew steadily, and his great desire was now for heaven.

He had achieved his goal on earth and was preparing for the last and greatest journey—to his eternal homeland.

After ten months in the novitiate, Stanislaus became very sick, but this time he was not afraid. He had his fellow novices and the kind Jesuit priests praying for him and assisting him.

He kept thinking how beautiful the Blessed Mother had been when she had brought Jesus to him. Now he asked Mary to bring *him* to *Jesus:* "Mother, on the next celebration of the Feast of your Assumption, please take me to heaven to be with you!"

In the early morning hours of the Feast of the Assumption, 1568, Stanislaus whispered to Father Ruitz that he saw the Blessed Virgin with many angels. At three o'clock in the morning he quietly died, at age eighteen.

The Blessed Mother had answered his prayer and granted his request to be admitted into heaven. Stanislaus had walked a total of fifteen hundred miles to give his life to God, and God had now brought him to Himself, to join the glory of the saints, in the company of his dear Blessed Mother.

"I see the Blessed Virgin with many angels!
She has come for me!"

Then...

Stanislaus' brother, Paul, made so many stops on his way to Rome that, even though he was *not* traveling on foot, he did not arrive until a month after Stanislaus' death.

When Paul began to ask whether anyone knew his brother, he was startled with the news: "Stanislaus is dead. He died a month ago, and all Rome is calling him the Polish saint."

With great sorrow filling his heart, Paul went to his brother's tomb. He cried bitterly over the cruel way he had treated him.

Then Paul changed his own way of life to one of goodness, and willingly testified to the virtues of his eighteen-year-old brother when he was asked to do so. At the age of sixty—after a long, repentant life—Paul asked for admission to the Society of Jesus.

Stanislaus was canonized in 1726.

St. Stanislaus had always longed for his homeland, heaven. When something pleasant happens, let us think that heaven will be much more wonderful, and let us say a prayer, asking our Lady to help us reach it.

Daughters of St. Paul

ALASKA
750 West 5th Ave., Anchorage, AK 99501 **907-272-8183.**
CALIFORNIA
3335 Motor Ave., W. Los Angeles, CA 90034 **213-202-8144.**
1570 Fifth Ave. (at Cedar Street), San Diego, CA 92101 **619-232-1442.**
46 Geary Street, San Francisco, CA 94108 **415-781-5180.**
CONNECTICUT
Bridgeport: Please check your phone book for current listing.
FLORIDA
2700 Biscayne Blvd., Miami, FL 33137 **305-573-1618.**
HAWAII
1143 Bishop Street, Honolulu, HI 96813 **808-521-2731.**
ILLINOIS
172 North Michigan Ave., Chicago, IL 60601 **312-346-4228; 312-346-3240.**
LOUISIANA
423 Main Street, Baton Rouge, LA 70802 **504-343-4057; 504-336-1504.**
4403 Veterans Blvd., Metairie, LA 70006 **504-887-7631; 504-887-0113.**
MASSACHUSETTS
50 St. Paul's Ave., Jamaica Plain, Boston, MA 02130 **617-522-8911.**
Rte. 1, 450 Providence Hwy., Dedham, MA 02026 **617-326-5385.**
MISSOURI
1001 Pine Street (at North 10th), St. Louis, MO 63101 **314-621-0346.**
NEW JERSEY
Hudson Mall, Route 440 and Communipaw Ave.,
Jersey City, NJ 07304 **201-433-7740.**
NEW YORK
625 East 187th Street, Bronx, NY 10458 **212-584-0440.**
59 East 43rd Street, New York, NY 10017 **212-986-7580.**
78 Fort Place, Staten Island, NY 10301 **718-447-5071; 718-447-5086.**
OHIO
616 Walnut Street, Cincinnati, OH 45202 **513-421-5733.**
2105 Ontario Street (at Prospect Ave.), Cleveland, OH 44115
216-621-9427.
PENNSYLVANIA
1719 Chestnut Street, Philadelphia, PA 19103 **215-568-2638;
215-864-0991.**
SOUTH CAROLINA
243 King Street, Charleston, SC 29401 **803-577-0175.**
TEXAS
114 Main Plaza, San Antonio, TX 78205 **512-224-8101.**
VIRGINIA
1025 King Street, Alexandria, VA 22314 **703-549-3806.**
WASHINGTON
2301 Second Ave. (at Bell), Seattle, WA 98121 **206-441-4100.**
CANADA
3022 Dufferin Street, Toronto 395, Ontario, Canada.